NICHOLA ROBERTS

The Story of St. Valentine

History of God's Brave Loving Servant | Patron Saint of Love and Relationships

Copyright © 2024 by Nichola Roberts

All rights reserved. No part of this publication may be reproduced, stored or transmitted in any form or by any means, electronic, mechanical, photocopying, recording, scanning, or otherwise without written permission from the publisher. It is illegal to copy this book, post it to a website, or distribute it by any other means without permission.

First edition

*This book was professionally typeset on Reedsy.
Find out more at reedsy.com*

Contents

Introduction		iv
1	Origin of Valentine's Day	1
2	Historical Context	4
3	Evolution of Valentine's Day Traditions	8
4	Patron Saint of Love	11
5	Valentine's Day Around the World	14
6	Symbols and Symbols of Love	20
7	Love and Relationships Beyond Valentine's Day	24
8	eflections on Love and Its Celebrations	30
9	Conclusion	34

Introduction

Every February 14th, the world collectively celebrates love, affection, and romance in the form of Valentine's Day. It's a day marked by the exchange of heartfelt sentiments, tokens of affection, and expressions of devotion. Yet, beyond the chocolates, flowers, and elaborate gestures, lies a rich tapestry of history, legend, and cultural significance that has woven the holiday into the fabric of society.

The origins of Valentine's Day are shrouded in mystery, with various theories and legends vying for prominence. One popular belief traces its roots back to ancient Rome, where the festival of Lupercalia was celebrated in mid-February to honor the Roman god of fertility, Lupercus. This pagan celebration involved rituals of purification and fertility, including the pairing of young men and women through a lottery system. Over time, as Christianity spread throughout the Roman Empire, the early Church sought to Christianize pagan holidays, and Lupercalia was eventually replaced by the feast day of St. Valentine.

The identity of St. Valentine himself is a subject of debate among historians, as there were several martyrs named Valentine who lived during the same period in the early Christian era. The most widely recognized figure is St. Valentine of Rome, a priest who defied Emperor Claudius II's decree prohibiting marriage for young men, believing that single men made better soldiers. Despite the risk of persecution, St. Valentine continued to perform marriages in secret, earning him the title of the patron saint of love.

As the legend of St. Valentine grew, so too did the association of his feast day with love and romance. Over time, the traditions of Valentine's Day evolved, incorporating elements from various cultures and historical periods. In medieval Europe, it became customary for lovers to exchange handmade cards and tokens of affection on Valentine's Day. These early "valentines" were often adorned with romantic verses and symbols of love, laying the foundation for the modern-day greeting card industry.

The commercialization of Valentine's Day gained momentum in the 19th century with the mass production of printed cards and the emergence of the floral and confectionery industries. The Victorian era saw a surge in the popularity of elaborate valentines adorned with lace, ribbons, and intricate designs, reflecting the era's emphasis on sentimentality and romance. Today, Valentine's Day is big business, with retailers capitalizing on the holiday to sell everything from flowers and chocolates to jewelry and romantic getaways.

But amidst the commercial hype, Valentine's Day remains a deeply personal and meaningful occasion for many people around the world. It's a time to express affection for loved ones, whether romantic partners, family members, or close friends. The holiday transcends cultural boundaries, with variations of Valentine's Day celebrated in countries across the globe, each with its own unique customs and traditions.

In literature and art, Valentine's Day has inspired countless works that explore the complexities of love and relationships. From Shakespearean sonnets to classic love stories, the theme of love has been a perennial favorite among writers and artists throughout history. Whether celebrating the joy of newfound love or lamenting the pain of unrequited affection, these works serve as poignant reminders of love's enduring power and universal appeal.

In the digital age, Valentine's Day has taken on new dimensions with the rise of social media, online dating, and virtual communication. Technology has transformed the way we express affection and connect with others, enabling us to share our love and appreciation instantly across vast distances. From virtual hugs to heartfelt messages sent via text or email, technology has made it easier than ever to celebrate love in all its forms.

As we embark on this exploration of Valentine's Day, let us delve into the rich tapestry of history, legend, and tradition that has made this holiday a beloved and cherished part of our cultural heritage. Whether you're a hopeless romantic or a skeptic of commercialized sentimentality, there's something for everyone to discover and appreciate about Valentine's Day and the enduring power of love. So, let us journey together through the pages of this book, as we uncover the mysteries and marvels of St. Valentine and his enduring legacy of love.

1

Origin of Valentine's Day

The roots of Valentine's Day trace back to the ancient Roman festival of Lupercalia, a pagan celebration held in mid-February to honor Lupercus, the god of fertility. Lupercalia was a raucous affair, marked by feasting, revelry, and fertility rituals aimed at ensuring bountiful crops and healthy livestock. Central to the festivities were the Luperci, a group of priests clad in goatskins, who would run through the streets of Rome, striking bystanders with strips of goat hide believed to bestow fertility and ward off evil spirits.

Over time, as Christianity gained traction throughout the Roman Empire, the early Church sought to supplant pagan holidays with Christian ones, thereby facilitating the conversion of the populace. In the 5th century, Pope Gelasius I declared February 14th to be the feast day of St. Valentine, effectively replacing Lupercalia with a Christian observance. However, the exact origins of St. Valentine and the connection to romantic love remain shrouded in mystery and legend.

One of the most enduring legends associates St. Valentine with acts of defiance against Emperor Claudius II's decree prohibiting marriage for young men. According to this legend, St. Valentine, a Roman priest, continued to perform marriages in secret, believing that love and marriage were sacred bonds ordained by God. When his clandestine activities were discovered, St. Valentine was arrested and imprisoned. During his incarceration, he purportedly fell in love with the jailer's daughter and sent her a love letter signed "from your Valentine" before his execution.

Another legend suggests that St. Valentine was a compassionate figure who ministered to Christians persecuted under the Roman Empire. Imprisoned for his faith, St. Valentine is said to have performed miracles, including healing the blind daughter of his jailer. Before his martyrdom, St. Valentine reportedly sent a letter to the young girl signed "from your Valentine," thus establishing the tradition of sending love notes on Valentine's Day.

Despite the ambiguity surrounding St. Valentine's true identity and the veracity of these legends, his feast day became synonymous with love and romance in the medieval period. In Geoffrey Chaucer's 14th-century poem "Parlement of Foules," Valentine's Day is associated with the mating season of birds and the renewal of love. Chaucer writes, "For this was sent on Seynt Valentyne's day / Whan every foul cometh ther to choose his mate."

By the 18th century, exchanging handmade cards and tokens of affection had become a popular Valentine's Day tradition in England. These early valentines were adorned with lace, ribbons, and sentimental verses, often crafted by hand and exchanged between lovers and friends. The tradition spread to the United States in the 19th century, fueled by advancements in printing technology and the burgeoning postal system. Mass-produced valentines became increasingly elaborate, featuring intricate designs and romantic imagery.

The commercialization of Valentine's Day accelerated in the 20th century with the rise of the greeting card industry and the marketing of flowers, chocolates, and other romantic gifts. Today, Valentine's Day is celebrated around the world with varying customs and traditions, from the exchange of love notes and gifts to romantic dinners and marriage proposals.

While the commercial aspects of Valentine's Day often overshadow its deeper significance, the holiday remains a time to celebrate love and affection in all its forms. Whether expressing devotion to a romantic partner, showing appreciation for friends and family, or simply indulging in self-love, Valentine's Day serves as a poignant reminder of love's enduring power to uplift and inspire. So, as we commemorate Valentine's Day each year, let us remember the ancient origins and timeless traditions that have made this holiday a cherished and beloved part of our cultural heritage.

2

Historical Context

To understand the significance of Valentine's Day within the broader historical context, it's essential to explore the societal norms, cultural practices, and religious beliefs that have shaped the celebration of love throughout the ages.

Dating back to ancient times, expressions of love and affection have been an integral part of human civilization. In ancient Egypt, love was idealized in poetry and literature, with romantic relationships depicted in art and inscriptions on temple walls. Similarly, the ancient Greeks celebrated love through their mythology, which featured gods and goddesses associated with romance and desire, such as Aphrodite, the goddess of love, and Eros, the god of erotic love.

In the classical world, the concept of romantic love evolved alongside societal changes and philosophical ideas. The Greek philosopher Plato explored the nature of love in his dialogues, distinguishing between physical desire (eros) and spiritual love (agape). Meanwhile, the Roman poet Ovid penned his "Ars

Amatoria" (The Art of Love), offering advice on courtship and seduction in ancient Rome.

With the spread of Christianity in the Roman Empire, the celebration of love took on new dimensions as the early Church sought to incorporate pagan festivals into the Christian calendar. In the 5th century, Pope Gelasius I declared February 14th to be the feast day of St. Valentine, thereby Christianizing the ancient Roman festival of Lupercalia. Over time, the traditions of Valentine's Day merged with Christian beliefs, leading to the association of St. Valentine with love and romance.

During the Middle Ages, Valentine's Day gained popularity as a day for courtly love, a concept rooted in the chivalric ideals of knighthood and courtly romance. Troubadours and minstrels composed songs and poems extolling the virtues of romantic love, often addressing their beloved as a noble and unattainable figure. Courtly love rituals, such as the exchange of love tokens and secret messages, became commonplace among the nobility of medieval Europe.

The Renaissance period witnessed a flourishing of art and literature that celebrated love and human emotions. Italian poets like Petrarch and Dante immortalized their unrequited love affairs in sonnets and epic poems, while painters like Botticelli and Titian depicted scenes of romance and passion in their artworks. The printing press, invented by Johannes Gutenberg in the 15th century, facilitated the mass dissemination of romantic literature and imagery, further popularizing the ideals of courtly love and romantic sentiment.

By the 18th century, Valentine's Day had become a widespread cultural phenomenon in England, marked by the exchange of handwritten love notes and tokens of affection. The industrial revolution brought about significant changes in society, including advancements in printing technology that enabled the mass production of valentines and greeting cards. The Victorians, known for their sentimentality and romanticism, embraced the tradition of sending elaborate valentines adorned with lace, ribbons, and romantic motifs.

In the United States, Valentine's Day gained popularity in the 19th century with the rise of the postal system and the emergence of the greeting card industry. Esther Howland, known as the "Mother of the American Valentine," began producing handmade valentines in the 1840s, which she sold through her Worcester, Massachusetts, business. Her elaborate designs, featuring lace, ribbons, and colorful illustrations, set the standard for modern valentine cards.

Throughout the 20th century, Valentine's Day continued to evolve as a commercialized holiday, with retailers capitalizing on the sale of flowers, chocolates, and romantic gifts. The advent of the internet and digital communication further transformed the way people express love and affection, with online dating platforms and social media networks facilitating connections between individuals worldwide.

Today, Valentine's Day remains a beloved and cherished holiday celebrated by people of all ages and backgrounds. Whether exchanging heartfelt greetings with loved ones, indulging in romantic gestures, or simply enjoying the company of friends and family, Valentine's Day serves as a reminder of the enduring power of love to inspire, uplift, and unite us as human beings.

3

Evolution of Valentine's Day Traditions

The celebration of Valentine's Day has undergone a fascinating evolution over the centuries, shaped by changing cultural norms, religious influences, and commercial interests.

Dating back to ancient Rome, the festival of Lupercalia provided the foundation for Valentine's Day, with its emphasis on fertility rites and matchmaking rituals. As Christianity spread throughout the Roman Empire, the early Church sought to Christianize pagan holidays, leading to the establishment of St. Valentine's feast day on February 14th. Over time, the traditions of Lupercalia merged with Christian beliefs, giving rise to the association of St. Valentine with love and romance.

During the Middle Ages, Valentine's Day became synonymous with courtly love, a concept rooted in the ideals of chivalry and nobility. Troubadours and minstrels composed songs and poems extolling the virtues of romantic love, while knights and ladies exchanged tokens of affection and secret messages. The rituals of courtly love, such as the giving of flowers and love letters, became popular among the nobility of medieval Europe.

The Renaissance period witnessed a flourishing of art and literature that celebrated love and human emotions. Italian poets like Petrarch and Dante immortalized their unrequited love affairs in sonnets and epic poems, while painters like Botticelli and Titian depicted scenes of romance and passion in their artworks. The printing press, invented by Johannes Gutenberg in the 15th century, facilitated the mass dissemination of romantic literature and imagery, further popularizing the ideals of courtly love and romantic sentiment.

By the 18th century, Valentine's Day had become a widespread cultural phenomenon in England, marked by the exchange of handwritten love notes and tokens of affection. The industrial revolution brought about significant changes in society, including advancements in printing technology that enabled the mass production of valentines and greeting cards. The Victorians, known for their sentimentality and romanticism, embraced the tradition of sending elaborate valentines adorned with lace, ribbons, and romantic motifs.

In the United States, Valentine's Day gained popularity in the 19th century with the rise of the postal system and the emergence of the greeting card industry. Esther Howland, known as the "Mother of the American Valentine," began producing handmade valentines in the 1840s, which she sold through her Worcester, Massachusetts, business. Her elaborate designs, featuring lace, ribbons, and colorful illustrations, set the standard for modern valentine cards.

Throughout the 20th century, Valentine's Day continued to evolve as a commercialized holiday, with retailers capitalizing on the sale of flowers, chocolates, and romantic gifts. The advent of the internet and digital communication further transformed the way people express love and affection, with online dating platforms and social media networks facilitating connections between individuals worldwide.

Today, Valentine's Day remains a beloved and cherished holiday celebrated by people of all ages and backgrounds. Whether exchanging heartfelt greetings with loved ones, indulging in romantic gestures, or simply enjoying the company of friends and family, Valentine's Day serves as a reminder of the enduring power of love to inspire, uplift, and unite us as human beings.

4

Patron Saint of Love

Saint Valentine, the patron saint of love, is one of the most celebrated figures in Christian history, revered for his steadfast devotion to love and romance. While the details of his life are shrouded in legend and myth, the legacy of St. Valentine has endured for centuries, inspiring countless lovers and romantics around the world.

St. Valentine's association with love and romance dates back to ancient Rome, where he served as a priest during the reign of Emperor Claudius II. According to popular legend, Claudius issued a decree forbidding young men from marrying, believing that single men made better soldiers. However, St. Valentine defied the emperor's orders and continued to perform marriages in secret, believing that love and marriage were sacred bonds ordained by God.

St. Valentine's clandestine activities eventually caught the attention of Roman authorities, and he was arrested and imprisoned for his defiance. While in jail, St. Valentine reportedly performed miracles, including healing the blind daughter of his jailer. Before his execution, St. Valentine is said to have sent a letter to the young girl signed "from your Valentine," thus establishing the tradition of sending love notes on Valentine's Day.

Another version of the legend suggests that St. Valentine was martyred for his refusal to renounce his faith in Christ and worship the Roman gods. While awaiting execution, St. Valentine befriended his jailer's daughter and prayed for her healing, leading to her conversion to Christianity. On the day of his execution, St. Valentine reportedly left her a note expressing his love and signed it "from your Valentine."

Over time, the stories of St. Valentine's martyrdom became intertwined with the traditions of Valentine's Day, transforming him into the patron saint of love and affection. In the Middle Ages, St. Valentine's feast day on February 14th became associated with courtly love, a concept rooted in the ideals of chivalry and nobility.

During the Victorian era, Valentine's Day evolved into a popular holiday marked by the exchange of handmade cards and tokens of affection. The Victorians, known for their sentimentality and romanticism, embraced the tradition of sending elaborate valentines adorned with lace, ribbons, and romantic motifs.

In the modern era, Valentine's Day has become a global celebration of love, celebrated by people of all ages and backgrounds. From exchanging heartfelt greetings with loved ones to indulging in romantic gestures and gestures of affection,

Valentine's Day serves as a reminder of the enduring power of love to inspire, uplift, and unite us as human beings.

As the patron saint of love, St. Valentine continues to inspire lovers and romantics around the world, symbolizing the timeless ideals of devotion, sacrifice, and affection. Whether commemorating his feast day with traditional rituals or simply expressing love and appreciation for those closest to us, St. Valentine's legacy reminds us of the profound significance of love in our lives.

5

Valentine's Day Around the World

Valentine's Day is celebrated in various ways around the world, with each culture adding its own unique customs and traditions to the holiday.

In the United States, Valentine's Day is typically associated with romantic love and is celebrated with the exchange of cards, flowers, and chocolates between romantic partners. It's also a day to express love and appreciation for family members and friends through heartfelt messages and gestures of affection.

In England, Valentine's Day has a long-standing tradition of sending anonymous love notes or "valentines." These cards often feature romantic verses and whimsical illustrations, and they're exchanged between secret admirers or between couples as a playful expression of affection.

In Japan, Valentine's Day is celebrated in a unique way, with a twist on traditional gender roles. On February 14th, women typically give chocolates to men, including friends, colleagues, and romantic interests. There are different types of chocolates given, ranging from "obligation chocolates" (giri-choko) for friends and coworkers to "true love chocolates" (honmei-choko) for romantic partners. A month later, on March 14th, known as White Day, men reciprocate by giving gifts to the women who gave them chocolates on Valentine's Day.

In South Korea, Valentine's Day is celebrated similarly to Japan, with women giving chocolates to men on February 14th. However, there's an additional twist: April 14th, known as Black Day, is designated for singles to mourn their solo status by eating black bean paste noodles (jajangmyeon) together. It's a lighthearted way for singles to commiserate and potentially meet new people.

In Brazil, Valentine's Day is celebrated on June 12th, known as Dia dos Namorados (Lovers' Day). It's a day for couples to exchange gifts, go out for romantic dinners, and celebrate their love. In addition to romantic partners, friends also exchange small gifts and cards as a token of appreciation for their friendship.

In Finland and Estonia, Valentine's Day is known as Ystävänpäivä (Friendship Day) and is celebrated as a day to honor friendships rather than romantic relationships. Friends exchange cards and small gifts to show appreciation for each other, and it's seen as an opportunity to strengthen social bonds and reconnect with loved ones.

These are just a few examples of the cultural variations in how Valentine's Day is celebrated around the world. Whether it's a day for romantic love, friendship, or both, Valentine's Day serves as a reminder of the importance of love, connection, and appreciation in our lives.

Customs and Traditions

Valentine's Day is celebrated around the world with a variety of customs and traditions that reflect the diverse cultures and beliefs of different societies.

One of the most common customs associated with Valentine's Day is the exchange of greeting cards, known as valentines. These cards often feature romantic imagery, such as hearts, flowers, and Cupid, and may include sentimental verses expressing love and affection. In some cultures, people also exchange gifts, such as flowers, chocolates, and jewelry, as tokens of their affection for their loved ones.

In many countries, Valentine's Day is also a popular occasion for romantic dinners and outings. Restaurants may offer special Valentine's Day menus or promotions, and couples often take the opportunity to enjoy a romantic meal together. Some couples also choose to celebrate Valentine's Day with a weekend getaway or a romantic trip, creating lasting memories together.

Another common tradition associated with Valentine's Day is the giving of flowers, particularly roses. Red roses are often associated with romantic love and passion, making them a popular choice for Valentine's Day gifts. However, other flowers, such as tulips, lilies, and orchids, are also commonly given as symbols of love and affection.

In addition to romantic gestures, Valentine's Day is also a time to celebrate friendships and platonic relationships. In some cultures, friends exchange small gifts or cards to show appreciation for each other, while others may host Valentine's Day parties or gatherings to celebrate the bonds of friendship.

For children, Valentine's Day is often celebrated in schools with classroom parties and the exchange of valentines among classmates. Children may decorate Valentine's Day cards with colorful designs and stickers, and some schools may organize Valentine's Day-themed crafts and activities to engage students in the spirit of the holiday.

In recent years, technology has also played a role in shaping Valentine's Day customs and traditions. Social media platforms allow people to share messages of love and affection with their friends and followers, while online shopping makes it easier than ever to find and send Valentine's Day gifts to loved ones near and far.

Overall, Valentine's Day is a time to celebrate love, affection, and connection with the people who matter most in our lives. Whether through romantic gestures, acts of kindness, or simple expressions of appreciation, Valentine's Day traditions serve to strengthen relationships and bring joy to both the giver and the recipient.

orde

Valentine's Day is celebrated around the world with diverse

customs and traditions that reflect the cultural richness and diversity of different societies. While the essence of the holiday remains the celebration of love and affection, the ways in which Valentine's Day is observed vary from country to country.

In the United States, Valentine's Day is a widely celebrated holiday, marked by the exchange of greeting cards, flowers, and chocolates between romantic partners. It's also a day for expressing love and appreciation for family members and friends, with many people sending cards and gifts to their loved ones.

In the United Kingdom, Valentine's Day has a long-standing tradition of sending anonymous love notes or "valentines." These cards often feature romantic verses and whimsical illustrations, and they're exchanged between secret admirers or between couples as a playful expression of affection. Valentine's Day is also celebrated with romantic dinners and outings, as well as the exchange of flowers and gifts.

In Japan, Valentine's Day is celebrated in a unique way, with a twist on traditional gender roles. On February 14th, women typically give chocolates to men, including friends, colleagues, and romantic interests. There are different types of chocolates given, ranging from "obligation chocolates" (giri-choko) for friends and coworkers to "true love chocolates" (honmei-choko) for romantic partners. A month later, on March 14th, known as White Day, men reciprocate by giving gifts to the women who gave them chocolates on Valentine's Day.

In South Korea, Valentine's Day is also celebrated similarly to

Japan, with women giving chocolates to men on February 14th. However, there's an additional twist: April 14th, known as Black Day, is designated for singles to mourn their solo status by eating black bean paste noodles (jajangmyeon) together. It's a lighthearted way for singles to commiserate and potentially meet new people.

In Brazil, Valentine's Day is celebrated on June 12th, known as Dia dos Namorados (Lovers' Day). It's a day for couples to exchange gifts, go out for romantic dinners, and celebrate their love. In addition to romantic partners, friends also exchange small gifts and cards as a token of appreciation for their friendship.

In Finland and Estonia, Valentine's Day is known as Ystävänpäivä (Friendship Day) and is celebrated as a day to honor friendships rather than romantic relationships. Friends exchange cards and small gifts to show appreciation for each other, and it's seen as an opportunity to strengthen social bonds and reconnect with loved ones.

These are just a few examples of the global celebrations of Valentine's Day. From romantic gestures to expressions of friendship and appreciation, Valentine's Day serves as a universal reminder of the importance of love, connection, and relationships in our lives.

6

Symbols and Symbols of Love

Roses, Chocolates, and Gifts

Roses have long been a symbol of love and romance, revered for their beauty, fragrance, and delicate petals. In many cultures, the giving of roses is a time-honored tradition on Valentine's Day, symbolizing deep affection, passion, and devotion. Red roses, in particular, are associated with romantic love and are often given as a token of admiration and desire. However, roses of different colors can convey different meanings; for example, pink roses symbolize gratitude and appreciation, while white roses signify purity and innocence.

Chocolates have also become synonymous with Valentine's Day, offering a sweet indulgence to mark the occasion. Chocolate's association with love and romance dates back centuries, with ancient civilizations like the Aztecs and Mayans valuing chocolate for its aphrodisiac properties. Today, chocolate is often given as a gift on Valentine's Day, with heart-shaped boxes and decadent assortments being popular choices. Whether milk, dark, or white chocolate, the sweetness and richness of chocolate are seen as a delicious expression of affection and appreciation.

Gift-giving is another cherished tradition on Valentine's Day, allowing people to express their love and appreciation for their partners, family members, and friends. From thoughtful tokens of affection to lavish gestures of romance, gifts come in all shapes and sizes, reflecting the unique tastes and preferences of both the giver and the recipient. Common Valentine's Day gifts include jewelry, perfume, clothing, and personalized items, as well as experiences such as spa days, romantic getaways, and special outings. Whether extravagant or simple, the act of giving and receiving gifts on Valentine's Day serves as a tangible expression of love, care, and thoughtfulness.

Heart Symbolism

The heart has been a symbol of love, affection, and emotion for centuries, transcending cultural and linguistic barriers to become universally recognized as a representation of the human capacity for love and compassion.

Throughout history, the heart has been associated with the seat of emotions and the source of love. In ancient cultures, such as those of the Egyptians and Greeks, the heart was believed to be the center of the soul and the essence of a person's being. This belief laid the foundation for the heart's symbolic significance in matters of love and emotion.

The heart's distinctive shape—a symmetrical, rounded form

with a cleft at the top and a pointed bottom—has become iconic in its representation of love and romance. The heart shape is often depicted in various contexts, from art and literature to advertising and branding, serving as a visual shorthand for matters of the heart.

In addition to its association with romantic love, the heart symbolizes a range of emotions and virtues, including compassion, kindness, and empathy. The phrase "heartfelt" is often used to describe emotions or actions that are sincere, genuine, and deeply felt, emphasizing the heart's connection to authenticity and sincerity.

The heart symbol is also closely linked to concepts of connection and unity. The image of two hearts intertwined or joined together represents the bond between individuals, whether romantic partners, family members, or friends. This symbolism underscores the idea of love as a unifying force that brings people together and fosters deep connections.

In religious and spiritual contexts, the heart holds additional significance as a symbol of devotion, faith, and spiritual awakening. In Christianity, for example, the Sacred Heart of Jesus is a symbol of divine love and compassion, representing Christ's unconditional love for humanity. Similarly, in Hinduism and Buddhism, the heart chakra is believed to be the center of love, compassion, and spiritual growth, aligning with the broader symbolism of the heart as a source of divine and transcendent love.

Overall, the heart symbolizes the profound capacity for love and emotion that defines the human experience. Its universal appeal and enduring significance make it a powerful symbol of connection, compassion, and the transformative power of love in all its forms.

7

Love and Relationships Beyond Valentine's Day

Building Strong Partnerships

Building strong partnerships, whether in personal relationships, business ventures, or collaborative projects, requires dedication, communication, trust, and mutual respect. Here are key principles to consider:

Clear Communication: Open and honest communication is essential for building trust and understanding between partners. Encourage transparent discussions about goals, expectations, and concerns to foster a supportive and collaborative environment.

Shared Vision: Establishing a shared vision or common goals provides a sense of purpose and direction for the partnership. Work together to define objectives, priorities, and strategies to achieve mutual success.

Mutual Respect: Respect for each other's opinions, ideas, and boundaries is fundamental to a healthy partnership. Value each other's contributions and perspectives, and strive to create an inclusive and supportive atmosphere.

Trust and Reliability: Trust is the foundation of any strong partnership. Demonstrate reliability, integrity, and accountability in your actions, and honor your commitments to build trust and confidence in the relationship.

Collaborative Problem-Solving: Address challenges and conflicts proactively by working together to find mutually beneficial solutions. Approach problems as opportunities for growth and learning, and seek input and feedback from all partners involved.

Flexibility and Adaptability: Recognize that partnerships may evolve over time and require flexibility to accommodate changing circumstances or priorities. Stay open to new ideas, opportunities, and ways of working together to adapt to changing needs and circumstances.

Celebrating Successes: Acknowledge and celebrate achievements, milestones, and successes together as a team. Recognize the contributions of each partner and take pride in your collective accomplishments.

Continuous Improvement: Commit to ongoing learning and growth as partners by seeking feedback, evaluating performance, and identifying areas for improvement. Strive for continuous improvement and innovation to strengthen the partnership over time.

Resilience: Building strong partnerships requires resilience and perseverance in the face of setbacks or challenges. Stay committed to the partnership and remain resilient in overcoming obstacles together.

Cultivating Empathy and Understanding: Foster empathy and understanding by actively listening to each other, practicing empathy, and considering each other's perspectives and experiences. Cultivate a culture of empathy and compassion to nurture strong and supportive partnerships.

By prioritizing clear communication, mutual respect, trust, collaboration, and continuous improvement, partners can build strong and resilient partnerships that withstand challenges and foster mutual growth and success over time.

Communication and Connection

Communication and connection are essential elements in fostering strong relationships and partnerships, whether in personal or professional settings.

Effective communication involves more than just exchanging information; it encompasses listening, understanding, and expressing oneself in a way that promotes clarity, empathy, and connection. Open and honest communication builds trust, enhances collaboration, and fosters a sense of mutual respect and understanding between individuals.

Connection goes beyond mere interaction; it involves establishing a meaningful bond or rapport with others based on shared values, interests, and experiences. Cultivating connection requires genuine interest, empathy, and active engagement in building relationships with others.

Through communication, individuals share thoughts, feelings, and ideas, creating opportunities for mutual understanding and connection. Whether through verbal or nonverbal means, communication allows people to express themselves, express empathy, and build rapport with others.

Connection, on the other hand, involves establishing a sense of rapport, trust, and mutual understanding with others. It requires genuine interest, empathy, and active engagement in building relationships based on shared values, interests, and experiences.

Together, communication and connection form the foundation of strong and meaningful relationships. By fostering open and honest communication, individuals can express themselves authentically, share their thoughts and feelings, and build trust and understanding with others. Cultivating connection involves actively engaging with others, demonstrating empathy, and building rapport based on shared experiences and interests.

In both personal and professional relationships, effective communication and connection are essential for building trust, fostering collaboration, and nurturing strong and meaningful connections that contribute to mutual growth, success, and fulfillment.

Nurturing Love Year-Round

Nurturing love year-round involves cultivating and maintaining a deep connection and affection for your partner throughout the different seasons of life. Here are some ways to nurture love consistently:

Regular Communication: Make communication a priority in your relationship by regularly sharing your thoughts, feelings, and experiences with your partner. This can include meaningful conversations, sharing laughter, and actively listening to each other.

Quality Time Together: Set aside dedicated time to spend with your partner, whether it's going on dates, enjoying shared hobbies, or simply spending quiet moments together. Quality time fosters intimacy and strengthens the bond between partners.

Acts of Kindness: Show your love and appreciation for your partner through small acts of kindness and gestures of affection. This can include writing love notes, cooking a special meal, or surprising them with thoughtful gifts.

Expressing Gratitude: Express gratitude for your partner's presence in your life and acknowledge the ways in which they enrich your life. Regularly express appreciation for their efforts, support, and contributions to the relationship.

Physical Affection: Physical touch is an important aspect of nurturing love in a relationship. Show affection through hugs, kisses, cuddling, and other forms of physical intimacy to strengthen the emotional connection between you and your partner.

Shared Goals and Dreams: Discuss your hopes, dreams, and aspirations with your partner and work together to create shared goals and plans for the future. Collaborating on shared goals fosters a sense of unity and teamwork in the relationship.

Respect and Support: Treat your partner with respect, kindness, and understanding, even during challenging times. Offer support and encouragement to your partner as they pursue their goals and navigate life's ups and downs.

Continual Growth and Learning: Be open to personal growth and development as individuals and as a couple. Continuously learn from each other, seek new experiences together, and adapt to changes in your relationship over time.

Celebrate Milestones and Achievements: Celebrate milestones, achievements, and special occasions together as a couple. Whether it's anniversaries, birthdays, or personal accomplishments, take time to acknowledge and celebrate each other's successes.

Forgiveness and Letting Go: Practice forgiveness and let go of grudges or resentments that may arise in your relationship. Choose empathy and understanding over judgment, and work through conflicts with compassion and respect.

By consistently nurturing love year-round through communication, quality time, acts of kindness, gratitude, physical affection, shared goals, respect, support, growth, celebration, and forgiveness, you can cultivate a strong, fulfilling, and enduring relationship with your partner.

8

eflections on Love and Its Celebrations

Love, in all its forms, is a profound and transformative force that shapes our lives and relationships in meaningful ways. As we reflect on love and its celebrations, we are reminded of the beauty, complexity, and significance of this universal human experience.

Love manifests itself in many different ways, from romantic love between partners to the deep bonds of friendship, familial love, and compassion for others. Each expression of love is unique and deeply personal, reflecting the depth of our emotions and the connections we share with others.

Love's celebrations, such as Valentine's Day and other special occasions, offer opportunities to honor and express our love for those who hold a special place in our hearts. These celebrations serve as reminders to cherish our relationships, express gratitude for the love we receive, and celebrate the bonds that unite us with others.

However, love is not confined to grand gestures or special occasions; it is present in the everyday moments of our lives, in the small acts of kindness, the shared laughter, and the quiet moments of connection with those we love. Love is found in the simple pleasures of spending time together, sharing experiences, and supporting each other through life's ups and downs.

As we celebrate love, we are also called to reflect on its complexities and challenges. Love requires vulnerability, patience, and effort to nurture and sustain over time. It requires us to communicate openly, to listen with empathy, and to work together to overcome obstacles and conflicts that arise in our relationships.

Love is not always easy, but it is worth the effort. It has the power to heal, to inspire, and to bring joy and fulfillment to our lives. Love teaches us to be compassionate, to be generous, and to see the beauty and worth in others.

In our reflections on love and its celebrations, let us remember to cherish the love we have been given, to express our love freely and openly, and to cultivate relationships built on mutual respect, understanding, and support. May we honor love in all its forms and celebrate the profound impact it has on our lives and the world around us.

Looking Forward to Future Valentine's Days

As we look forward to future Valentine's Days, we anticipate the opportunity to continue celebrating love and strengthening the bonds that unite us with our loved ones. With each passing year, we envision new experiences, shared moments, and expressions of affection that deepen our connections and enrich our lives.

We eagerly anticipate the chance to create more memories with our partners, family members, and friends, cherishing the traditions and rituals that bring us together on this special day. Whether it's exchanging heartfelt messages, enjoying romantic dinners, or simply spending quality time together, we look forward to embracing the love and warmth that Valentine's Day brings.

As we journey into the future, we envision growth and evolution in our relationships, as we navigate life's twists and turns together. We anticipate facing challenges and overcoming obstacles with resilience and grace, knowing that love is the foundation that sustains us through all of life's ups and downs.

We look forward to exploring new ways to express our love and appreciation for each other, discovering new traditions and rituals that reflect the unique dynamics of our relationships. Whether it's planning adventures, pursuing shared interests, or simply being present with each other, we eagerly anticipate the opportunities to deepen our connection and strengthen our bond.

As we look ahead to future Valentine's Days, we envision a lifetime of love, laughter, and shared experiences with those who mean the most to us. We embrace the opportunity to celebrate love in all its forms, honoring the relationships that bring joy, fulfillment, and meaning to our lives.

With each passing Valentine's Day, we renew our commitment to nurturing love, fostering connection, and cherishing the precious moments we share with our loved ones. As we journey into the future together, we look forward to celebrating love not just on Valentine's Day, but every day of the year.

9

Conclusion

In conclusion, the story of St. Valentine serves as a timeless reminder of the enduring power of love to inspire, unite, and transform lives. From its origins in ancient Rome to its evolution into a global celebration of love and affection, the legacy of St. Valentine continues to captivate hearts and minds around the world.

Through the centuries, Valentine's Day has evolved from a solemn religious observance to a vibrant cultural phenomenon, marked by the exchange of cards, gifts, and gestures of affection. Yet, at its core, Valentine's Day remains a testament to the enduring significance of love in human experience, transcending time, culture, and tradition.

The story of St. Valentine's devotion to love and romance serves as a poignant reminder of the profound impact that love can have on individuals and societies alike. Whether commemorating the martyrdom of a Christian saint or celebrating the joy of romantic connection, Valentine's Day offers an opportunity to reflect on the power of love to inspire, uplift, and unite us as human beings.

As we honor the legacy of St. Valentine and celebrate love in all its forms, may we be reminded of the importance of cherishing the relationships that enrich our lives, expressing gratitude for the love we receive, and embracing the profound beauty of the human heart. In doing so, we honor the spirit of St. Valentine and affirm the enduring significance of love as a guiding force in our lives.

Made in the USA
Coppell, TX
06 February 2025